THE ULTIMATE ANIMAL LIBRARY

White-tailed Deer

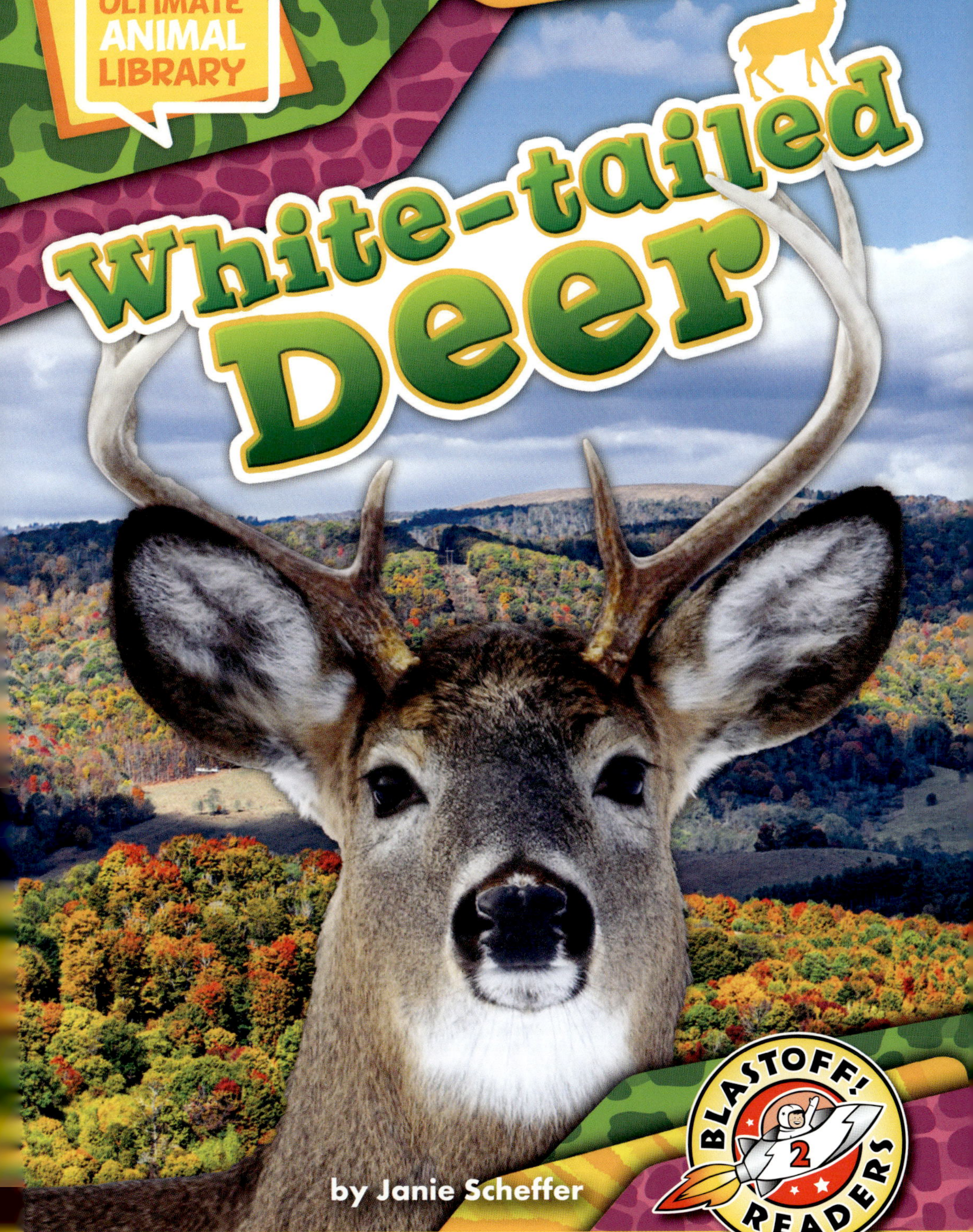

BLASTOFF! READERS 2

by Janie Scheffer

BELLWETHER MEDIA • MINNEAPOLIS, MN

Blastoff! Readers are carefully developed by literacy experts to build reading stamina and move students toward fluency by combining standards-based content with developmentally appropriate text.

Level 1 provides the most support through repetition of high-frequency words, light text, predictable sentence patterns, and strong visual support.

Level 2 offers early readers a bit more challenge through varied sentences, increased text load, and text-supportive special features.

Level 3 advances early-fluent readers toward fluency through increased text load, less reliance on photos, advancing concepts, longer sentences, and more complex special features.

★ **Blastoff! Universe**

Reading Level

Blastoff! Beginners — Grade K

Blastoff! Readers — Grades 1–3

Blastoff! Discovery — Grade 4

This edition first published in 2025 by Bellwether Media, Inc.

Library of Congress Cataloging-in-Publication Data

LC record for White-tailed Deer available at: https://lccn.loc.gov/2024038364

Editor: Elizabeth Neuenfeldt   Series Designer: Veah Demmin

Printed in the United States of America, North Mankato, MN.

Table of Contents

What Are White-tailed Deer?

White-tailed deer are **mammals**. They live in North America and South America. The underside of their tails is white. It is how they got their name!

White-tailed Deer Report

Range

Status in the Wild

Habitats

White-tailed deer **coats** change color with the seasons. The change helps them hide from **predators**.

They are reddish brown in summer.
They are grayish brown in winter.

These deer have a great sense of smell. They can smell when danger is near.

They also hear well.
Their ears move
in different directions.

Bucks grow **antlers** in summer. Bucks use their antlers to **spar** with one another. This happens during **mating season** each fall.

Bucks **shed** their antlers in winter.

Spot a White-tailed Deer

sparring

Run, Leap, Swim!

White-tailed deer live in forests and **prairies**. They are active at sunrise and sunset.

Many live alone. But some gather in small groups.

White-tailed deer are **herbivores**. They eat many different plants.

They are **ruminants**.
Their stomachs can
break down tough plants.

White-tailed deer can run around 30 miles (48.3 kilometers) per hour. They can leap high, too.

They are strong swimmers.
They swim away from predators.

Growing Up

Does give birth to one to three **fawns** at once. Fawns have white spots.

Fawns can walk at birth. They can eat plants shortly after they are born.

fawn

Fawns lose their spots as they grow. They leave mom within two years.

It is time to find their own food!

Life of a White-tailed Deer

Name of Babies

fawns

Number of Babies

1 to 3

Time Spent with Mom

1 to 2 years

Life Span

2 to 3 years

Glossary

antlers—branched bones on the heads of some animals; antlers look like horns.

bucks—male deer

coats—the hair or fur covering some animals

does—female deer

fawns—baby white-tailed deer

herbivores—animals that only eat plants

mammals—warm-blooded animals that have backbones and feed their young milk

mating season—the time of year when white-tailed deer join together to make young

prairies—large grasslands that are mostly flat and treeless

predators—animals that hunt other animals for food

ruminants—animals with three or four stomachs

shed—to lose something on the body; male white-tailed deer shed their antlers at the same time every year.

spar—to fight

To Learn More

AT THE LIBRARY

Jeffries, Corina. *Deer Make Mischief!* Buffalo, N.Y.: Enslow Publishing, 2024.

Kenney, Karen Latchana. *Forests.* Minneapolis, Minn.: Bellwether Media, 2022.

Murray, Tamika M. *Meet a Baby White-Tailed Deer.* Minneapolis, Minn.: Lerner Publications, 2024.

ON THE WEB

FACTSURFER

Factsurfer.com gives you a safe, fun way to find more information.

1. Go to www.factsurfer.com.
2. Enter "white-tailed deer" into the search box and click .
3. Select your book cover to see a list of related content.

Index

The images in this book are reproduced through the courtesy of: Jim Cumming, front cover, p. 15; Kristi Blokhin, front cover background, interior background; Collins Unlimited, front cover (deer icon); Richard R E, p. 3; Tony Campbell, pp. 4, 18-19; Ricardo Reitmeyer, p. 6; Amy Lutz, p. 7; Paul Tessier, pp. 8, 10-11; Denise Iacangelo, p. 9; Dennis W Donohue, p. 10; JAMES PIERCE, p. 11; Michael Tatman, p. 12; Thomas Pettengill, p. 13; Tom Reichner, pp. 14, 17 (white-tailed deer), 23; Mircea Costina, pp. 16-17; Derek R. Audette, p. 17 (coyotes); Karel Bartik, p. 17 (gray wolves); Evgeniyqw, p. 17 (mountain lions); Nick Pecker, p. 17 (shrubs); anmbph, p. 17 (trees); SakSa, p. 17 (nuts); Debbie Steinhausser, p. 18; Barbara Smits, p. 20; Barbara MacDonald, p. 21.